On the cover:

Black bears are the smallest and most common American bear. Not all black bears are black. They can range in color from blond to brown to black. Black bears are the only bears that now live in California. The grizzly bear, shown on the California state flag, no longer lives there.

A Reading/Language Arts Program

Program Authors

Diane August
Donald R. Bear
Janice A. Dole
Jana Echevarria
Douglas Fisher
David Francis
Vicki Gibson
Jan E. Hasbrouck
Scott G. Paris
Timothy Shanahan
Josefina V. Tinajero

Unit 4

Teamwork

Let's Team Up

THE BIG QUESTION

THEME: Teammates

THEME: Family Teams

THEME: Helping the Community

THEME: Better Together

THEME: Animal Teams

STANDARDS PRACTICE: Show What You Know

Unit 4

Let's Team Up

The Big Question

How do teams work together?

Theme Launcher Video

Find out more about teamwork at **www.macmillanmh.com.**

Teammates

Talk About It

What is a team? What kinds of teams do you know about?

LOG ON Find out more about being part of a team at **www.macmillanmh.com.**

Words to Know

- once
- upon
- saw
- eight
- across
- carry
- walked

- trip
- borrow

Read to Find Out

Will Snail find her way home?

Frog and Snail's Trip

Once **upon** a time, Frog **saw** a little snail. The snail looked sad.

"I was on a **trip** but now I am lost," said Snail.

"I have a map," said Frog.

"Can I **borrow** it?" asked Snail.

"Show me where you live," said Frog.

"I live over these **eight** hills and **across** that pond," said Snail.

"I will go with you," said Frog. "If you **carry** the map, I will carry the snacks."

So the two new friends **walked** to Snail's home together.

Comprehension

Genre

A **Folktale** is a story that has been told for many years.

Ask Questions

Make Predictions

Use your Predictions Chart.

What I Predict	What Happens

Read to Find Out

What happens when Drakes Tail goes to see the king?

Drakes Tail

retold by Ruby Bell
illustrated by Richard Bernal

Once upon a time, there was a duck named Drakes Tail.

Drakes Tail was a duck with brains. He saved all of his money. One day, the king asked to **borrow** some. The duck said yes.

Drakes Tail waited for the king to pay him back. But the king did not.

So Drakes Tail set off to see the king.

"Quack! Quack! Quack! Time to get my money back!" he sang.

On his way, Drakes Tail **saw** his friend Fox.

"Fox!" said Drakes Tail, "I am going to the king to get my money back!"

"Take me!" said Fox. "I can help!"

"OK," said Drakes Tail. "But the **trip** is long. You may get tired. Make yourself little and hop into my bag. I will **carry** you."

Fox did as the duck said.

"Quack! Quack! Quack! Time to get my money back!" sang Drakes Tail.

Then Drakes Tail saw his friend Pond.

"I am going to the king to get my money back," said Drakes Tail.

“May I go with you?” asked Pond.

“Yes,” said Drakes Tail. “But the trip is long. You may get tired. Make yourself little and hop into my bag.”

Pond did as the duck said.

"Quack! Quack! Quack! Time to get my money back!" sang Drakes Tail.

Drakes Tail spotted his friend Hive.

"I am going to the king to get my money back," said Drakes Tail.

Hive wished to come, too. So Hive got little and hopped into Drakes Tail's bag.

Drakes Tail **walked** **across** the land.

After **eight** days, he made it to the king's palace.

"Quack! Quack! Quack! Can I have my money back?" Drakes Tail asked the king.

But the king had spent it all!

"Stick that duck in the hen pen!" yelled the king.

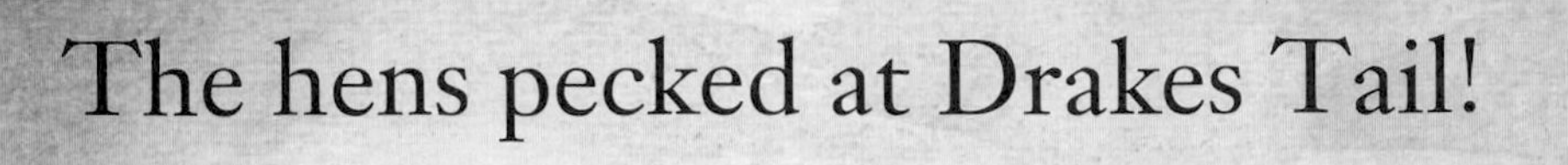

The hens pecked at Drakes Tail!

"Fox! Fox! I am in bad shape. Come and help me get out of this scrape!" sang Drakes Tail.

Fox hopped out of Drakes Tail's bag. He chased the hens away.

Drakes Tail went back to the king. "Quack! Quack! Quack! Can I have my money back?"

"That duck shall make a fine snack!" said the king. "Put him in a pot!"

“Pond! Pond! I am in a bad spot. Put out the fire that is so hot!” sang Drakes Tail.

Pond gushed out of the bag and put out the fire. Drakes Tail ran.

"Catch that duck!" yelled the king.

Drakes Tail sang, "Hive! Hive! Help me please! It is time to send out the bees!"

Hive sent its bees to sting the king and his men. They ran and ran.

Drakes Tail sat on the king's throne to rest. Just then, the people of the kingdom came in.

"Drakes Tail is a duck with brains. Let's make him our king!" they said.

Drakes Tail sang, "I will be the king today, if you say my friends can stay!"

From that day on, Drakes Tail ruled the kingdom. He had Fox, Pond, and Hive at his side.

Richard Bernal's Tale

Richard Bernal says, "I have always liked to illustrate old stories like *Drakes Tail*, to help make them seem new. I also love to illustrate birds. I often go to the zoo to take photographs of birds. It was a pleasure to create a little duck like Drakes Tail."

Other books by Richard Bernal

Find out more about Richard Bernal at **www.macmillanmh.com**.

Illustrator's Purpose

Richard Bernal likes to illustrate old stories. Draw a character from an old story you like. Write about your drawing.

Critical Thinking

Retell the Story

Use the Retelling Cards to retell the story in order.

Retelling Cards

Think and Compare

1. What did you predict would happen when Drakes Tail reached the kingdom? What did happen?

What I Predict	What Happens

2. Have your friends ever helped you as Drakes Tail's friends helped him? How?

3. Do you think Drakes Tail will make a good king? Why or why not?

4. How are Drakes Tail and his friends like Frog and Snail in "Frog and Snail's Trip"?

Busy As a Bee

Science

Genre
Nonfiction gives information about a topic.

Text Feature
A **Caption** gives information about a photograph or picture.

Content Vocabulary
worker
honey
queen

Find out more about animals at **www.macmillanmh.com.**

Buzz, buzz, buzz! Bees are at home in a hive. They are so busy! All of them have jobs that help the hive.

Bees can make a hive in a tree.

Worker bees make wax cups called honeycombs.

Lots of **worker** bees live in a hive. They make **honey**. They help the hive stay clean. They fan the hive with their wings when it gets hot.

Every hive has a **queen** bee. What is her job? She lays eggs.

A hive has drone bees, too. A drone's job is to help the queen make eggs.

A queen bee is with her drones in the hive.

The queen lays eggs inside wax cups.

New bees hatch from the eggs. The worker bees feed them.

As time passes, a hive can get quite big. Buzz, buzz, buzz! A big hive is a busy place!

Critical Thinking

- How are the bees acting as a team?
- How are they like Drakes Tail and his friends?

Writing

Was and Were

The verbs **was** and **were** tell about the past.

Write About Being on a Team

Carlos wrote about being on a kickball team.

We were playing kickball in Pine Park. After I kicked, I ran to all the bases. I was glad I helped the team!

Your Turn

Have you ever been on a team or worked with others?

Write about it.

Tell what you did and how you helped.

Writer's Checklist

- ☑ Did I write about being on a team?
- ☑ Did I use the verbs **was** and **were** correctly?
- ☑ Did I begin each special name with a capital letter?

Family Teams

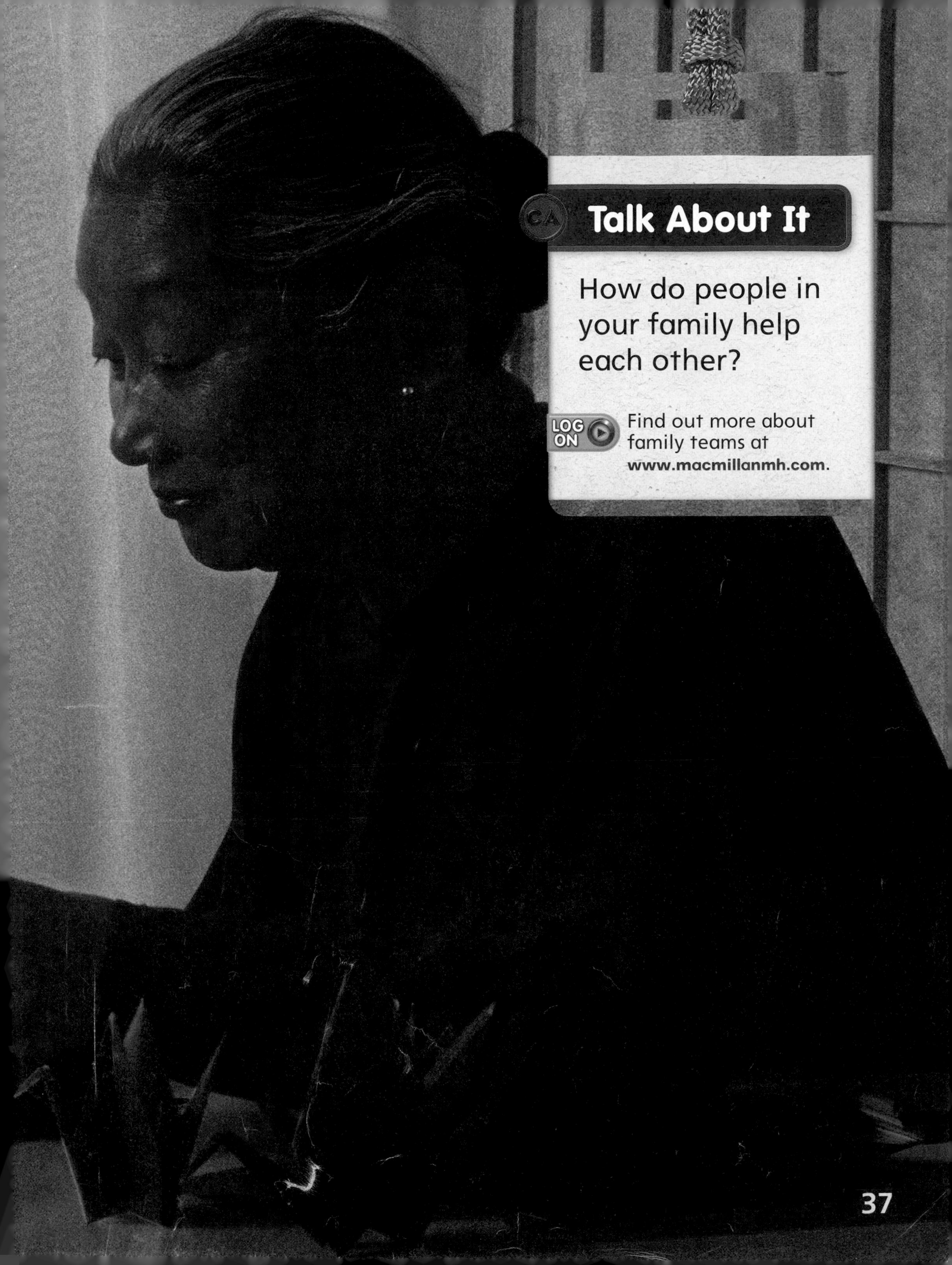

Talk About It

How do people in your family help each other?

LOG ON Find out more about family teams at **www.macmillanmh.com**.

Words to Know

- give
- were
- says
- pretty
- about
- write

- splendid
- concentrate

Read to Find Out

How does the girl feel about her big sister?

When Jean Comes Home

I like it when Jean comes home from school.

I **give** her a big hug. "You **were** away for so long!" I say.

"I missed you!" Jean **says**. She gives me a gift. It is a **pretty** doll.

Mom and Dad are glad to see Jean, too. "You look **splendid**," they say.

Jean tells us all **about** school. She has to read and **write** a lot. She has to **concentrate** to get her work done.

But now Jean is back home. "Do you want to play?" she asks me.

"Yes!" I say.

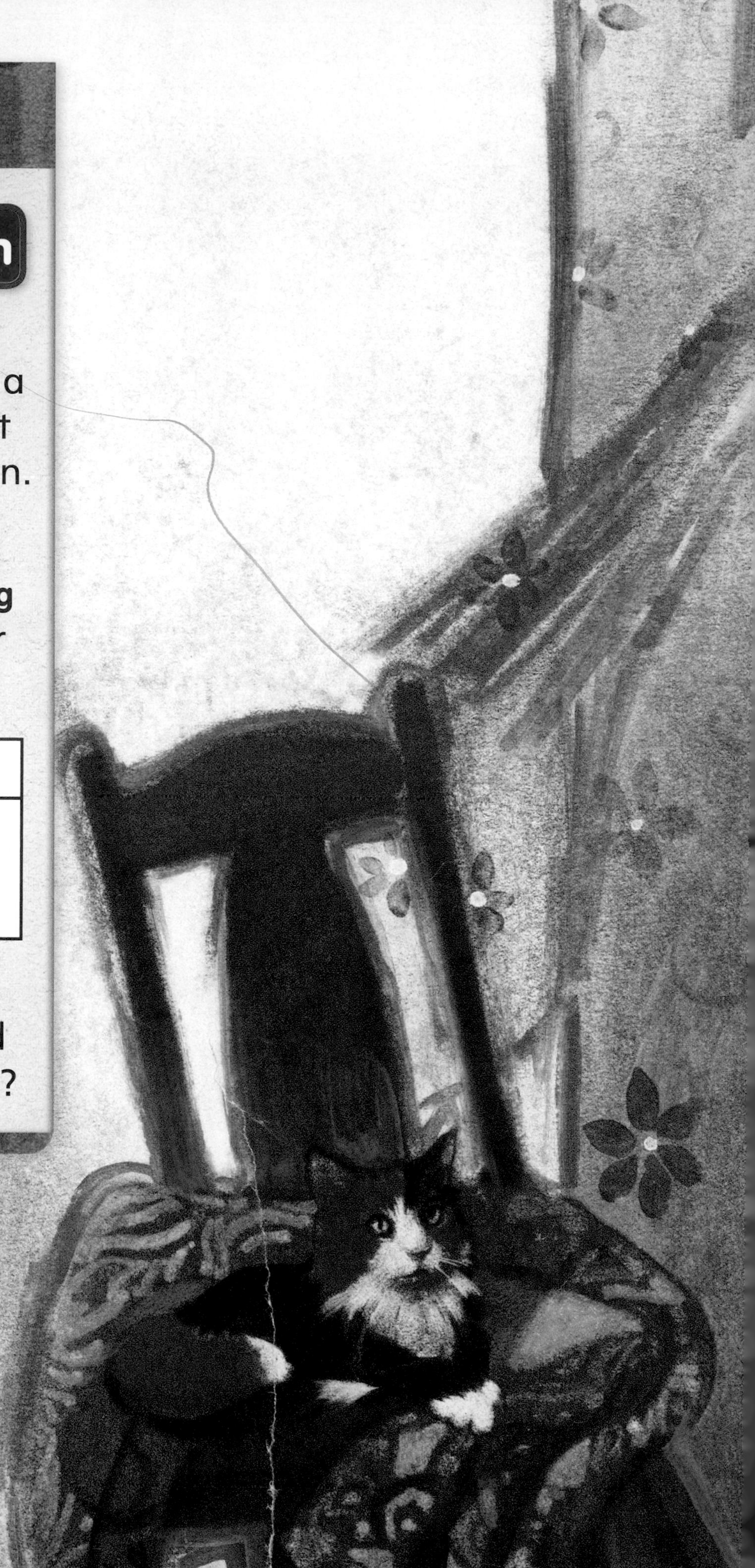

Comprehension

Genre

Realistic Fiction is a made-up story that could really happen.

Ask Questions

Character and Setting
Use your Character and Setting Chart.

What the Characters Do	Where They Do It

Read to Find Out

What do Gram and James do together?

Gram and Me

by Miriam Cohen
illustrated by Floyd Cooper

Award Winning Author and Illustrator

I like my grandmother a lot.
I call her Gram.
She is so much fun.

Gram takes me fishing.
We sit together on the dock.
We wave at the boats.
“Hello!” we call.

Gram helps me ride my bike.
It has two wheels.
"You can do it, James!" she **says**.
"Look at me go!" I say.

Gram has a cat named Bean.
Bean feels soft when I pet him.
"Scratch him under the chin," she says.
"Bean likes it!" I say.

Gram likes to play chess.
She helps me when we play.
"**Concentrate**, James," she says.
"I win, Gram!" I say.

Gram has a lot of **pretty** flowers.
She lets me **give** them a drink.
"Flowers need a good drink," she says.
"Look! They drank it all up," I say.

Gram has a big plum tree.
We like to pick plums.
Gram lifts me so I can reach them.
"I got a ripe one!" I say.

Gram teaches me how to make plum jam.
She adds salt to the pot.
“Just a bit,” she says.
“Yum! This jam will taste good!” I say.

"Gram, did you cook when you **were** little?" I ask.
"I helped my mom," says Gram. "We made jam just like you and I do."

"Did you go to school?" I ask.
"Yes, I went to a little school," says Gram.
"My school is very big," I say.
"Yes, it is," says Gram.

"I am learning to read and **write** at school,"
I say.
"That is good," says Gram. "I learned to read and write when I was just your age."
"Gram, can you read me a story?"

"Yes," says Gram. "Do you like cats and dogs?"

"I like them a lot!" I say.

"This is a story **about** cats and dogs."

I like Gram's story a lot.
"Let's read more," I say.
"Can you read a story to me?" asks Gram.
"I think I can."

"I will read you this story," I say.
"Is it about cats and dogs?" Gram asks.
"No, it is a story about pigs."
"Pigs are good, too," says Gram.

"This is a story about three little pigs," I say.
I read on and on.

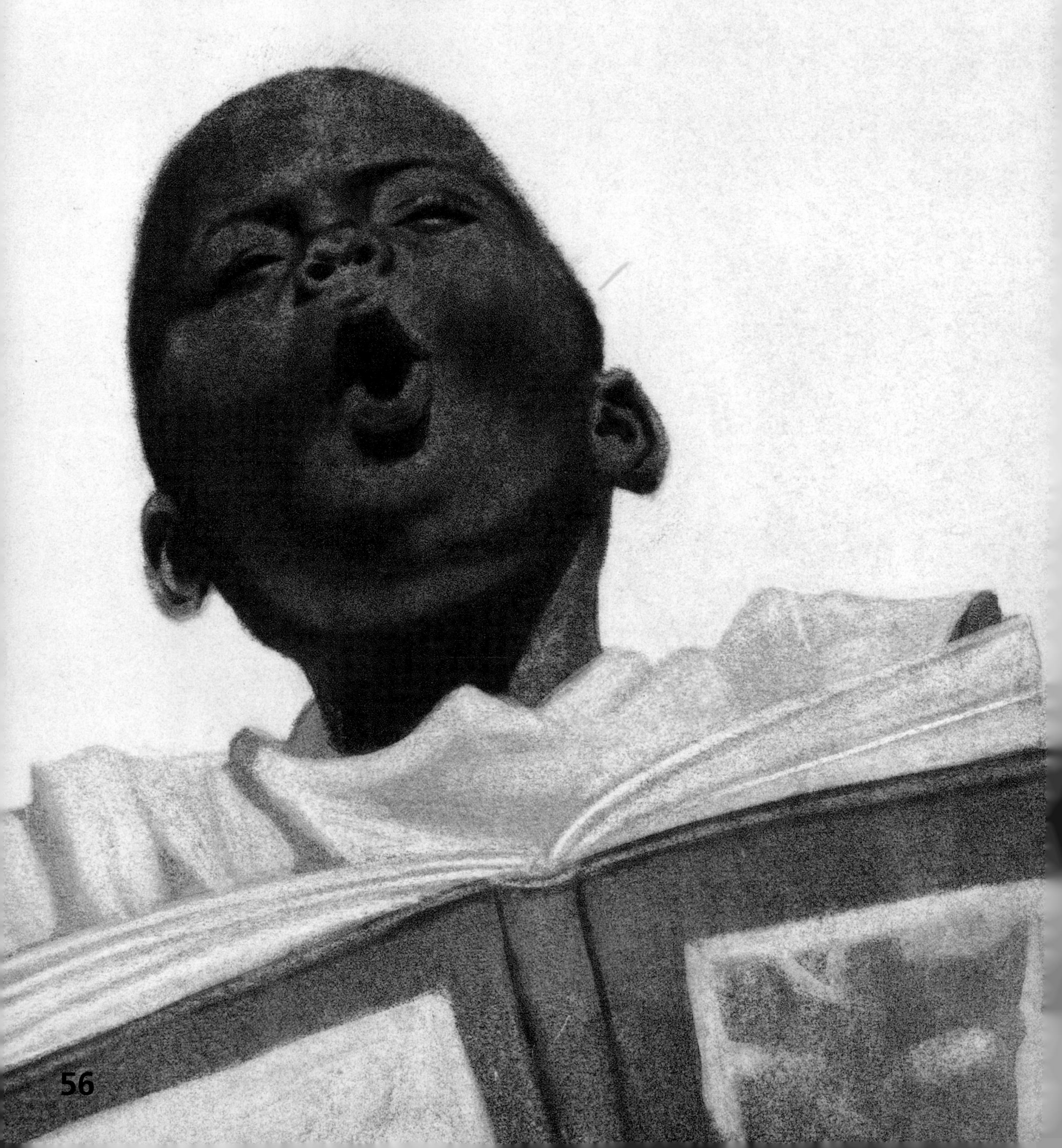

At the end, Gram claps and claps.
"What a **splendid** story," she says.
"Gram, you are so much fun," I say.
"So are you," says my Gram.

READ TOGETHER We Remember Gram

Miriam Cohen says, “I wrote this story about a grandma because I loved mine so much. She told me stories about when she was a girl.”

Another book
by Miriam Cohen

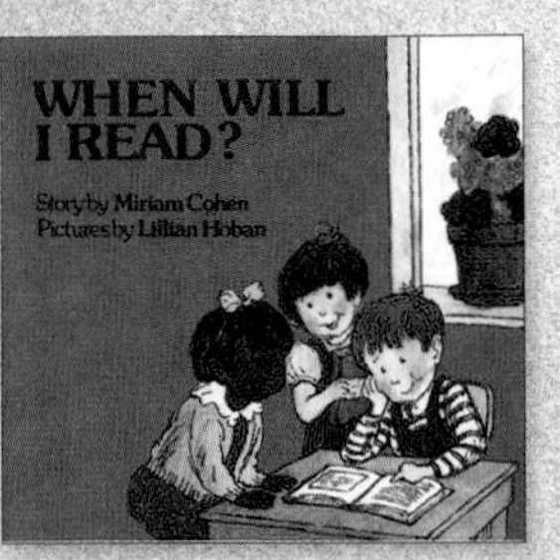

Floyd Cooper says, “I loved my gram’s gingerbread. I start my paintings by spreading gingerbread-colored paint on paper. So, I remember Gram every time I make a painting!”

LOG ON Find out more about Miriam Cohen and Floyd Cooper at **www.macmillanmh.com**.

Another book
by Floyd Cooper

Eloise Greenfield
GRANDPA’S FACE
Illustrated by Floyd Cooper

Author’s Purpose

Miriam Cohen wrote about her grandma. Write about a relative who is special to you.

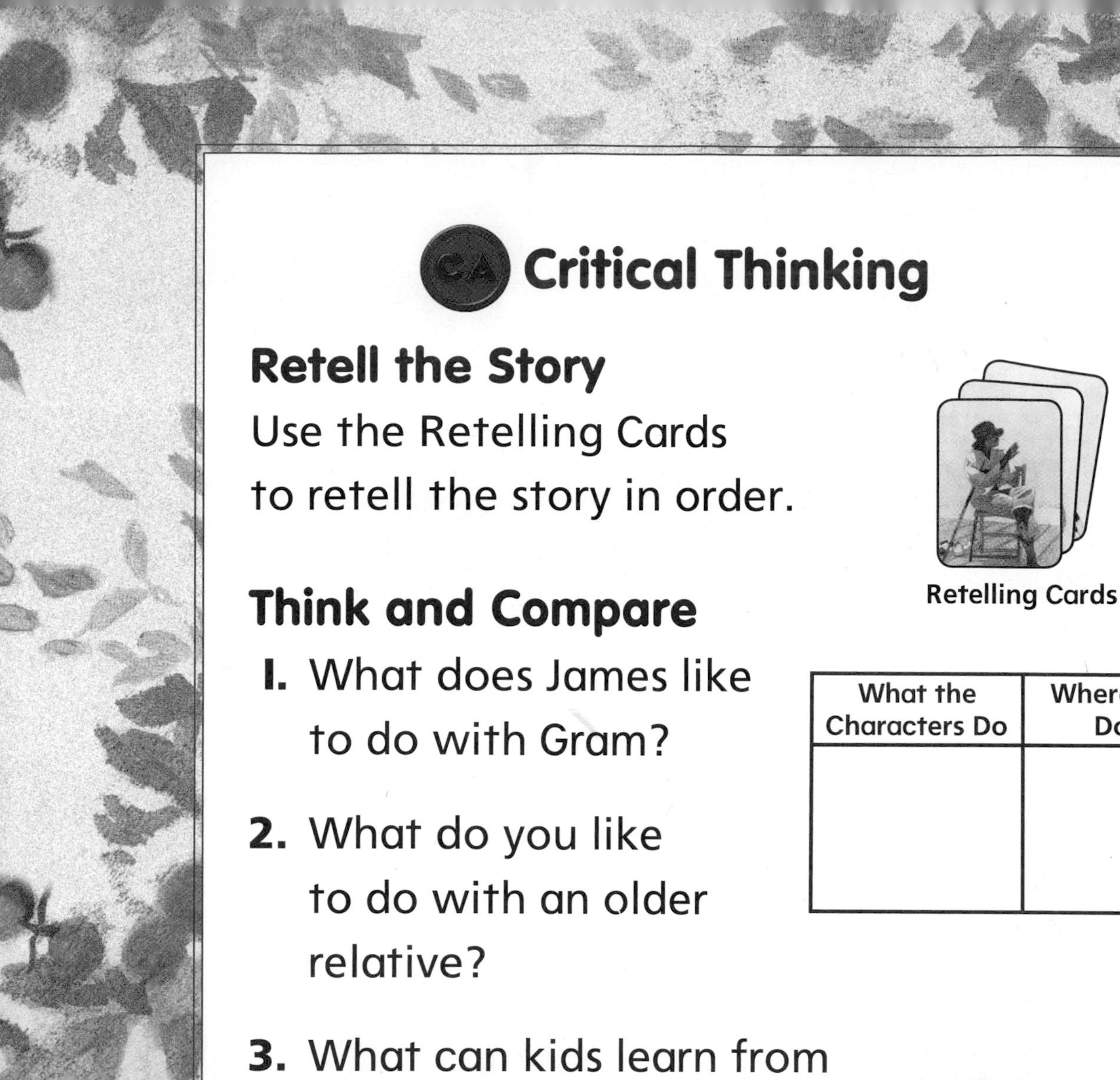

Critical Thinking

Retell the Story

Use the Retelling Cards to retell the story in order.

Retelling Cards

Think and Compare

1. What does James like to do with Gram?

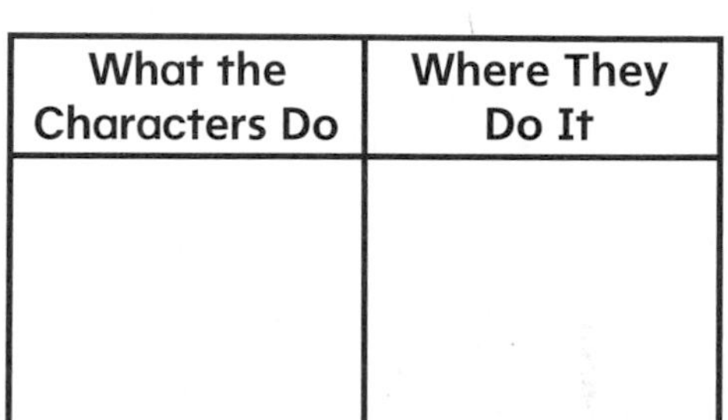

What the Characters Do	Where They Do It

2. What do you like to do with an older relative?

3. What can kids learn from older relatives?

4. How are James and the little sister in "When Jean Comes Home" alike?

Chinese New Year

History/ Social Science

Genre
Nonfiction tells about real people, places, and events.

Text Feature
A **Numerical List** is a series of things written in 1, 2, 3 order.

Content Vocabulary
celebrate
relatives
parade

LOG ON Find out more about Chinese traditions at **www.macmillanmh.com.**

Chinese New Year is a lot of fun. Let's see how kids **celebrate** it.

Things to Do

1. Make things to eat.
2. Make a costume.
3. Get a flag.
4. Get gifts.

To get set, Ming Lee makes a list.
She has a lot to do!

On the big day, Ming Lee and her mom and dad go to see **relatives**. They bring gifts. Kids like Ming Lee get red packets with money in them. They have good things to eat like New Year's cake.

The day ends in a big **parade**. People dress up. They wave big flags. What a fun way to start the year!

Critical Thinking

- How do you celebrate the new year?
- How might James and Gram from *Gram and Me* celebrate the new year?

Talk About It

How can we work together to make our community better?

Find out more about helping the community at **www.macmillanmh.com.**

THINK GREEN!

Helping the Community

TIME FOR KIDS

Words to Know

change
better
move
buy

ripe
difficult

Read to Find Out

How do peaches get picked?

Picking Peaches

We have peach trees. When the peaches are little, they are not good. But then they **change**. They are much **better** to eat when they grow.

Once the peaches are **ripe**, we must get to work. We have a **difficult** job. We work as a team. We **move** from tree to tree, picking as we go.

When you **buy** a peach, think about where it came from. Think about the people who picked your peach.

Comprehension

Genre

Nonfiction

A nonfiction article can tell about real people and events.

Reread

Retell

Retell what happens using your own words.

César Chávez

César Chávez was a great man. In his life, he helped a lot of people. He helped people who picked crops the most.

Farmers grow crops, such as grapes and peaches.

When the crops are **ripe**, they need to be picked. Then crop pickers come to pick the crops.

For a long time, these crop pickers had a **difficult** life. They picked crops in the hot sun all day. The farmers did not pay them much.

When there were no crops left,
the pickers had to **move**.

They had many homes each year.
But the homes were not good.
The crop pickers lived in shacks.

César Chávez did not like this. He wanted the crop pickers to have a **better** life. He felt that if people worked together, things could **change**.

Grapes were one of the biggest crops. César Chávez told the crop pickers not to pick grapes. He told people not to **buy** grapes.

The grapes began to rot.
The farmers did not like this.

The crop pickers marched with César Chávez. They spoke to the farmers. They asked for more pay. They asked for better homes.

◀ **César Chávez stands with grape pickers.**

It took a long time, but the farmers did make changes.

Today, crop pickers have a better life. They get more pay. They live in better homes. They thank César Chávez, who helped them work together.

Critical Thinking

Tell What You Learned

What did you learn about César Chávez?

Think and Compare

1. What made the crop pickers' life hard?
2. What crop would you like to grow? How do you think you could grow it?
3. How did César Chávez help the crop pickers?
4. What might César Chávez have said to the peach pickers in "Picking Peaches"?

CA

Show What You Know

Think and Search Find the answer in more than one place.

Grown in California

California has a lot of big farms. People all over eat crops grown on these farms. How can crops get to far away places? How can the crops stay fresh?

A long time ago they couldn't. But then trains were made. Crops could go fast in these trains. Cold cars kept the crops cold. That helped keep them fresh.

Today crops can go in trucks and on planes. Now people from many states can eat a peach, bean, or grape grown in California!

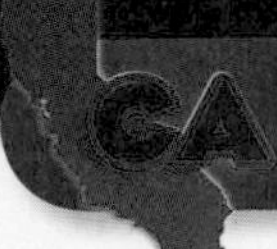

Directions: Answer the questions.

1 **How did crops first get across the country?**

A

B

C

2 **How did cold railroad cars help the crops?**

A They helped crops grow more.

B They helped crops stay fresh.

C They changed the color.

3 **Which kind of food is the story about?**

A bread

B fruits and vegetables

C cheese

Tip

Keep reading to find the answer.

STOP

Write About a Person You Admire

Crystal wrote about a lifeguard.

Julie is the lifeguard at my beach. She is a great swimmer. It is her job to help save lives. Last year she saved a boy. She likes her job a lot.

Your Writing Prompt

Think of a person you look up to. It could be a person you really know. It could be a person you have heard about.

Write a report telling about the person.

Writing Hints

- ✔ Tell why the person you admire is special.
- ✔ Write clearly so that readers will understand you.
- ✔ Check your report for mistakes.

Better Together

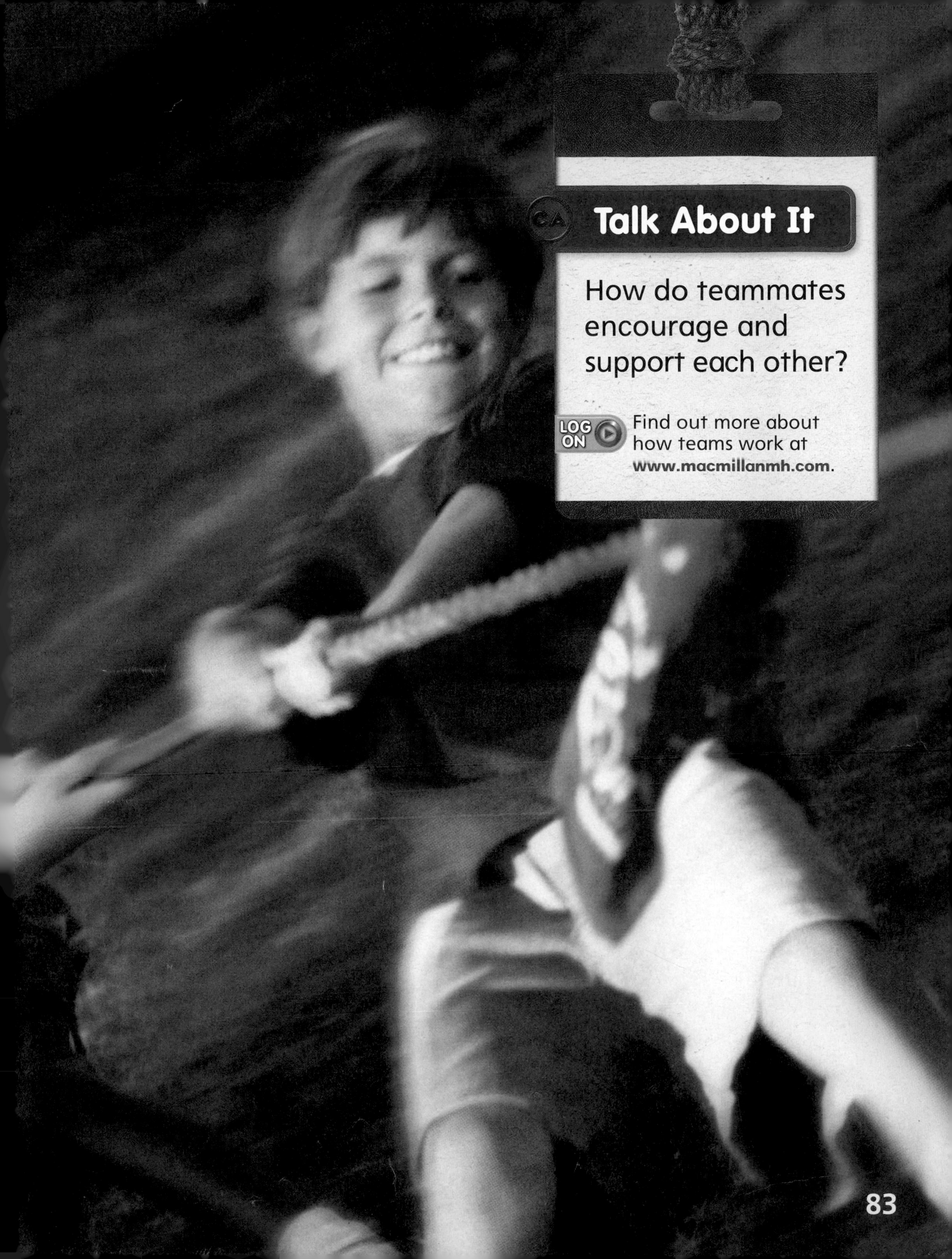

Talk About It

How do teammates encourage and support each other?

LOG ON Find out more about how teams work at www.macmillanmh.com.

Words to Know

- ball
- head
- should
- shout
- never

- perhaps
- meadow

Read to Find Out

What helps Little Cub hit the ball?

See the Ball Fly!

Little Cub is up at bat. He swings, but he misses the **ball**.

He puts his **head** down.

"Perhaps I **should** not be at bat," he thinks.

"You can do it, Little Cub!" **shout** his teammates.

On his next try, Little Cub hits the ball. He sees it fly over the **meadow**.

"I've **never** hit a ball that well!" he says to himself. Then he runs to each base.

Comprehension

Genre

A **Fantasy** is a made-up story that could not really happen.

Visualize

Problem and Solution

Use your Problem and Solution Chart.

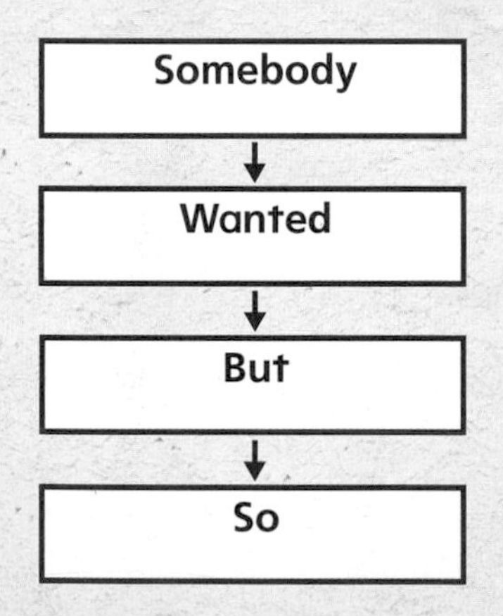

Read to Find Out

How will Frog and Toad fly the Kite?

The Kite

from Days with Frog and Toad

Award Winning Author and Illustrator

by Arnold Lobel

Frog and Toad went out
to fly a kite.
They went to
a large **meadow**
where the wind was strong.
"Our kite will fly up and up,"
said Frog.
"It will fly all the way up
to the top of the sky."

"Toad," said Frog,

"I will hold the **ball** of string.

You hold the kite and run."

Toad ran across the meadow.
He ran as fast as his short legs
could carry him.
The kite went up in the air.
It fell to the ground with a bump.
Toad heard laughter.
Three robins were sitting in a bush.

"That kite will not fly,"

said the robins.

"You may as well give up."

Toad ran back to Frog.

"Frog," said Toad,

"this kite will not fly.

I give up."

"We must make a second try,"

said Frog.

"Wave the kite over your **head**.

Perhaps that will make it fly."

Toad ran back across the meadow.

He waved the kite over his head.

The kite went up in the air

and then fell down with a thud.

"What a joke!" said the robins.

"That kite will **never**

get off the ground."

Toad ran back to Frog.

"This kite is a joke," he said.

"It will never get off the ground."

"We have to make

a third try," said Frog.

"Wave the kite over your head

and jump up and down.

Perhaps that will make it fly."

Toad ran across
the meadow again.
He waved the kite
over his head.
He jumped up and down.
The kite went up in the air
and crashed down into the grass.
“That kite is junk,”
said the robins.
“Throw it away and go home.”

Toad ran back to Frog.

"This kite is junk," he said.

"I think we **should**

throw it away and go home."

"Toad," said Frog,

"we need one more try.

Wave the kite over your head.

Jump up and down

and **shout** UP KITE UP."

Toad ran across the meadow.

He waved the kite over his head.

He jumped up and down.

He shouted, "UP KITE UP!"

The kite flew into the air.

It climbed higher and higher.

READ TOGETHER

Arnold Lobel's Story

Arnold Lobel was often sick and missed many days of school when he was young. When he went back to school, he made friends by telling stories and drawing pictures. Many years later, Lobel's children liked to catch frogs and toads. Lobel loved the animals and wrote about them in his Frog and Toad stories.

Other books by Arnold Lobel

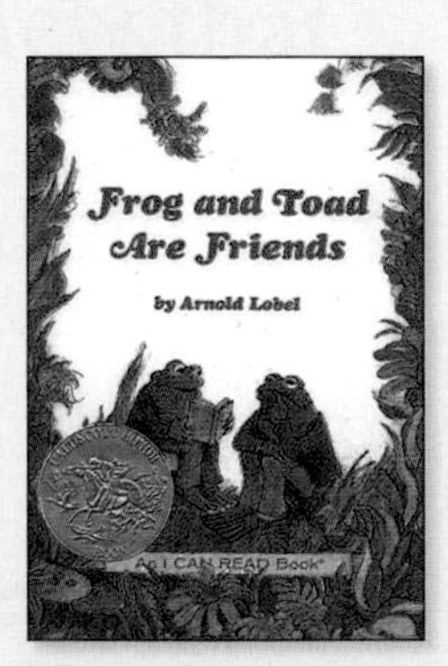

CA **Author's Purpose**

Arnold Lobel wanted to write about good friends. Write about your friend. Tell how you help each other.

Critical Thinking

Retell the Story

Use the Retelling Cards to retell the story in order.

Retelling Cards

Think and Compare

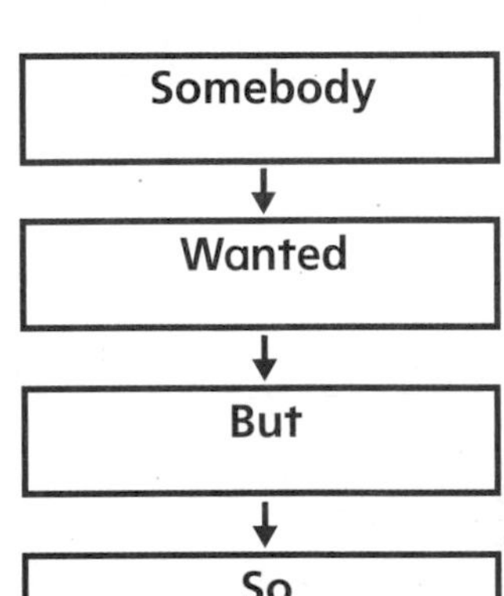

1. What problem do Frog and Toad have? How do they solve it?
2. How do you feel when you try to do something hard? How does Toad feel?
3. How do Frog and Toad act like friends?
4. What do Little Cub in "See the Ball Fly!" and Frog and Toad have in common?

History/
Social Science

Genre
Nonfiction gives information about a topic.

Text Feature
A Chart shows information in an organized way.

Content Vocabulary
invented
machine
airplane

Find out more about things that fly at **www.macmillanmh.com**.

The Wright Brothers

Wilbur and Orville Wright were brothers. People called them Will and Orv.

Will and Orv both liked to fix things. They liked to ride things, too.

Will and Orv liked bikes a lot. They had a bike shop.

Will and Orv had wheels. But they wanted wings. They wanted to fly.

In those days long ago, there were no planes. So Will and Orv got to work. First, they made a glider. A glider is like a kite that a person can ride on.

Will and Orv liked the glider. But they wanted it to do more. They saw birds use their wings and tails to help them go up and down and turn.

Will and Orv got to work. They **invented** a **machine**. It was the first **airplane**. The plane had propellers and an engine. These helped the plane move like a bird.

On a cold day in 1903, Will and Orv tried the plane. It went up! It stayed up for 12 seconds. That is not a lot, but it showed that the plane worked!

This is how we can get to places today. We can go on land, by water, and high up in the sky.

Thanks to Wilbur and Orville Wright, we can fly!

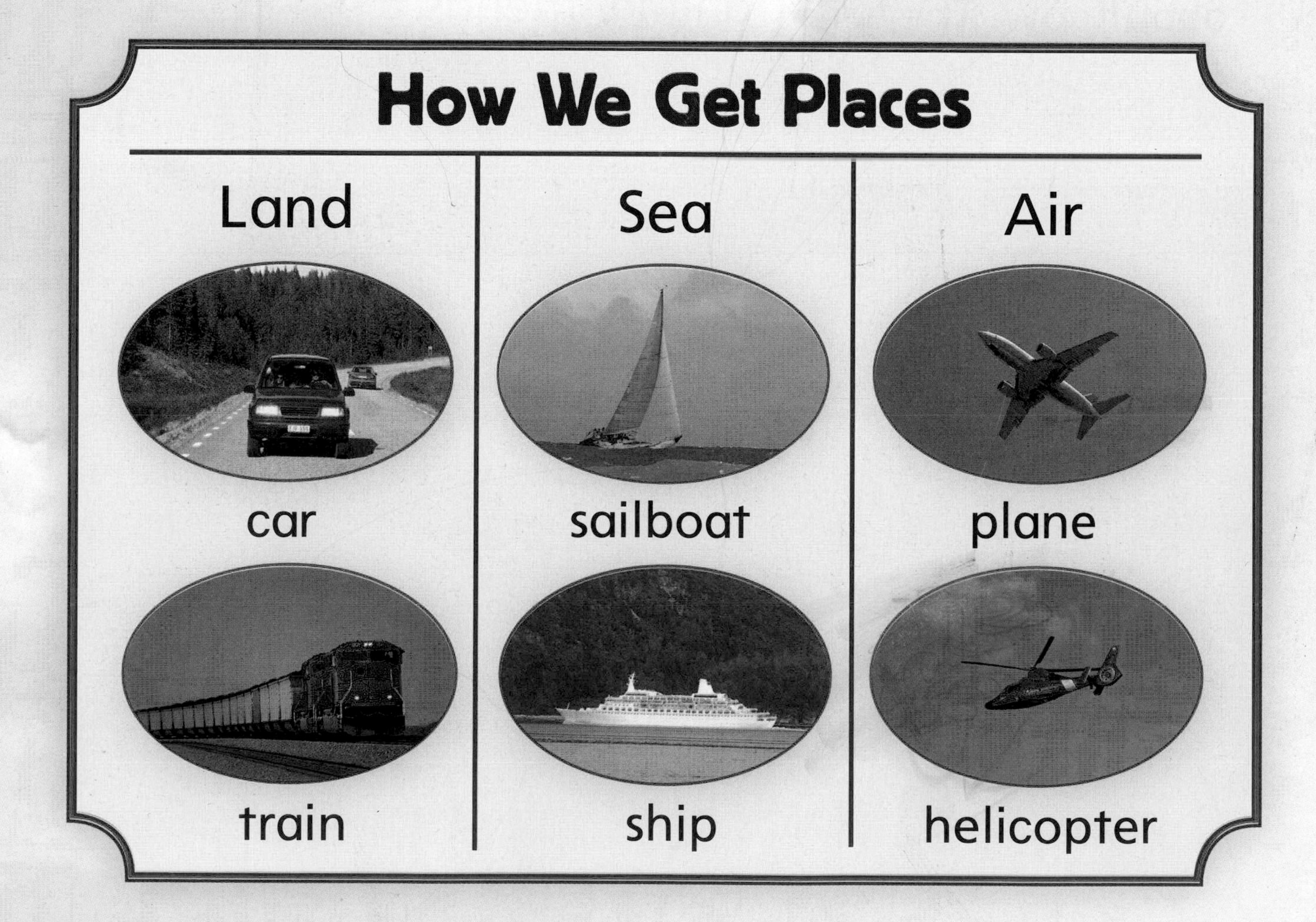

Critical Thinking

- How did the Wright brothers act like a team?
- How are Frog and Toad like the Wright Brothers?

Writing

See and Saw

The verb see tells about now. The verb saw tells about the past.

Write a Story

Skye wrote about animal friends.

Jake, the mouse, was hungry.
"I *saw* a nut on the tree yesterday," he said.
"I can *see* it now!" said a little bird.
"I will get it for you."
"Thank you!" said Jake.

Your Turn

Write a made-up story about friends.

Think about who the friends in your story are.

Tell how they could help each other.

Writer's Checklist

- ☑ Did I write about friends who help each other?
- ☑ Did I tell what the friends said and did?
- ☑ Did I use **see** and **saw** correctly?

Animal Teams

Talk About It

Do you think animals can help each other? How?

LOG ON Find out more about animal teams at **www.macmillanmh.com**.

Words to Know

- or
- because
- also
- other
- until
- blue

- danger
- beautiful

Read to Find Out

Why do fish swim together in a school?

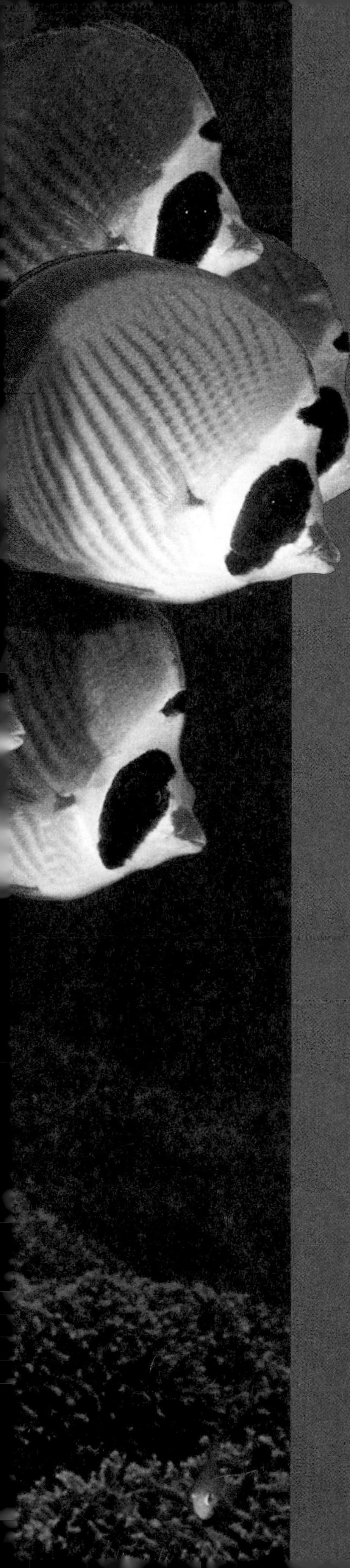

A School of Fish

Some fish swim together in a school. What is a school of fish? It is many big **or** little fish swimming in a bunch.

A school of fish works like a team. Many fish swimming together can see **danger** better than one fish. The fish swim in a school **because** they will be safer.

Fish in schools **also** can find more to eat. Why? It's because many, many fish are looking. All the fish look for plants or **other** good things. They look **until** they see what they like to eat.

So, in a lake or the **beautiful blue** sea, it helps fish to be in school!

Comprehension

Genre
Nonfiction gives information about a topic.

Text Structure
Retell
Use your Retelling Chart.

Retell

Read to Find Out
How do animals act as teams?

Main Selection

Animal Teams

By Rachel Mann

Can a little bird help a big giraffe?
Can a shrimp help a fish?

Yes, they can!

These might seem like funny friends. But many kinds of animals work together in teams. These animals help each **other** in lots of ways. Let's find out how.

Some birds live
on the backs of
big animals. Why
do the animals
let the birds stay?
The birds help.
They eat bugs off
the animals' skin.

The big animals help
the little birds, too.
The birds are safe on
top of these big pals.
And they are happy
because they have lots
of yummy bugs to eat!

The goby fish and the blind shrimp make a good team.

The shrimp can't see, so the goby helps. The goby looks out for **danger**, and the shrimp stays close. When the goby flicks its tail, it means that it is time to hide.

The shrimp helps the goby, too. It has a hole to hide in. It lets the goby hide there, too. The shrimp and the goby hide **until** it is safe to go out.

Zebras and wildebeests live on the hot, sunny plains. They both like to graze on grass all day.

These animals are seen together a lot. Why?

They stay together because they can help each other find fresh grass to eat.

They **also** help each other stay safe. If a zebra **or** a wildebeest spots danger, it runs. This tells the rest to run, too.

Many fish want to eat the little clown fish. It needs a safe home. So it lives in a sea anemone.

The clown fish is safe because most fish stay away. Why? The sea anemone stings! But the clown fish can not feel its sting.

The clown fish helps its buddy, too. It swims in and out, in and out. It chases away big fish that might hurt its pal.

A caterpillar needs to be safe so that it can grow.

Who will help? Ants will! They find the caterpillar and take it to a safe place.

Why do ants do this?

The caterpillar has a sweet liquid on its skin. The ants like the taste.

Soon the caterpillar will be a **beautiful blue** butterfly.

When a little cleaner fish is hungry, it looks for fish to clean. Why? It gets a free meal when it cleans.

A cleaner fish eats the pests off of other fish.

The fish want to be cleaned.
They line up and wait for the
cleaner fish to get to them.

One is big, and one is little.
But the two are friends.

When animals team up, they do what is best for both of them.

Join Rachel Mann's Team

Rachel Mann loves learning about animals, especially animals who act in unexpected ways. She really enjoyed researching and writing *Animal Teams* because she learned that animals help and need each other just as people do.

CA **Author's Purpose**

Rachel Mann likes to find out about animals who do interesting things. Write about an animal that does something you find interesting.

Critical Thinking

Retell the Story

Use the Retelling Cards to retell the selection in order.

Retelling Cards

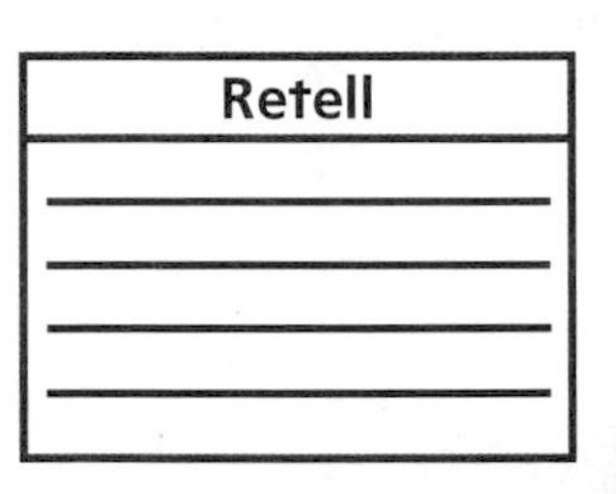

Think and Compare

1. How do the goby fish and the blind shrimp work as a team?

2. What animals have you seen together? How did they act?

3. Can you think of other pairs of animals that might make good teams? How could they help each other?

4. How are the animals in *Animal Teams* like the fish in "A School of Fish"?

Poetry

Genre
Poetry helps readers look at things they see every day in new ways.

Literary Element
Repetition is the way some words in a poem are used more than once to create an effect.

LOG ON Find out more about birds at **www.macmillanmh.com**.

READ TOGETHER

Where?

by Charlotte Zolotow

I look up into the sky
and see the birds
like black arrows
flying high.
Where they come from where they go
Only they really know
flying flying flying by
in the blueness of the sky.

Critical Thinking

- How are the birds in the poem acting like the animals in *Animal Teams*?
- Why do you think they are flying together?

Writing

Contractions

A **contraction** is a short form of two words.

does + not = doesn't

Write About an Animal Team

Sam wrote about animals from *Animal Teams*.

The shrimp digs a hole.
The goby can go in and stay safe.
The goby swims with the shrimp.
That way, the shrimp
doesn't get hurt.

Your Turn

Think of an animal team you know or have read about.

Write about the animals.

Tell how they work together.

Writer's Checklist

- [x] Did I write about animals that work as a team?
- [x] Did I explain clearly how they work together?
- [x] Did I use an apostrophe in place of an *o* in each **contraction** with *not*?

Review

Retell
Character and Setting
Labels
Captions
Contractions

Ray and His Bones

My dog Ray loves bones. One day when it snowed, Mom gave Ray a bone. He wagged his tail.

Ray held the bone in his teeth. He ran to the backyard. He dug a hole. Then he dropped in the bone and piled on snow.

All winter, Ray buried his bones in the snow. He buried bones from our meals. He buried bones from our friends' meals. In all, Ray buried nine bones!

How could we tell how many bones there were? That's easy. When the snow melted, we could see each one!

As Tall as the Trees

Giraffes are the tallest mammals. Long necks and legs help make them so tall. They have manes and little horns.

Giraffes can reach high with those long necks. They can eat the leaves at the tops of trees.

Giraffes get food and water from leaves.

A male giraffe is called a bull.
A bull can be nineteen feet tall.
A female giraffe is called a cow.
A cow can grow to be sixteen feet tall.
A baby giraffe is called a calf.
It is six feet tall at birth.

Read the labels that name some parts of a giraffe. Name more parts that you see.

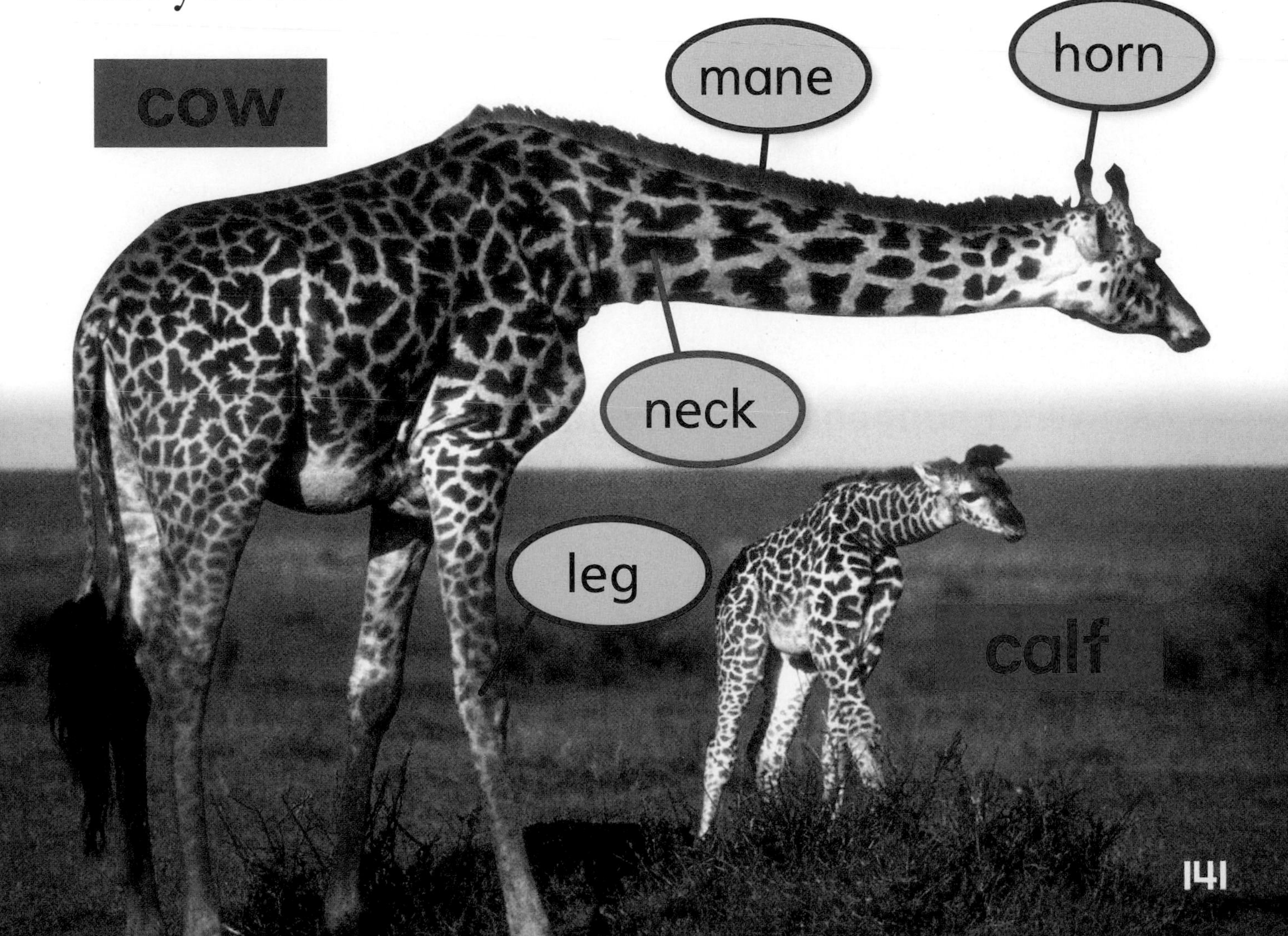

CA Critical Thinking

Now answer the questions. Base your answers on the story "Ray and His Bones."

1 What is the SETTING of this story?

A a boat

B a school

C a backyard

2 Which sentence describes Ray BEST?

A Ray likes to sleep and rest.

B Ray is a very little dog.

C Ray likes to play and dig.

3 What happened in "Ray and His Bones"? Write it in your own words.

Now answer the questions. Base your answers on the story "As Tall as the Trees."

1 **How do giraffes get water?**

A They get water from eating leaves.

B They live near lakes.

C People leave water in bowls.

2 **Which part of the giraffe does not have a label?**

A neck

B horn

C tail

Write on Demand

PROMPT What animals do you like to watch? What do you see? Write as much as you can and as well as you can.

Glossary

What Is a Glossary?

A glossary can help you find the meanings of words. The words are listed in alphabetical order. You can look up a word and read it in a sentence. Sometimes there is a picture.

Sample Entry

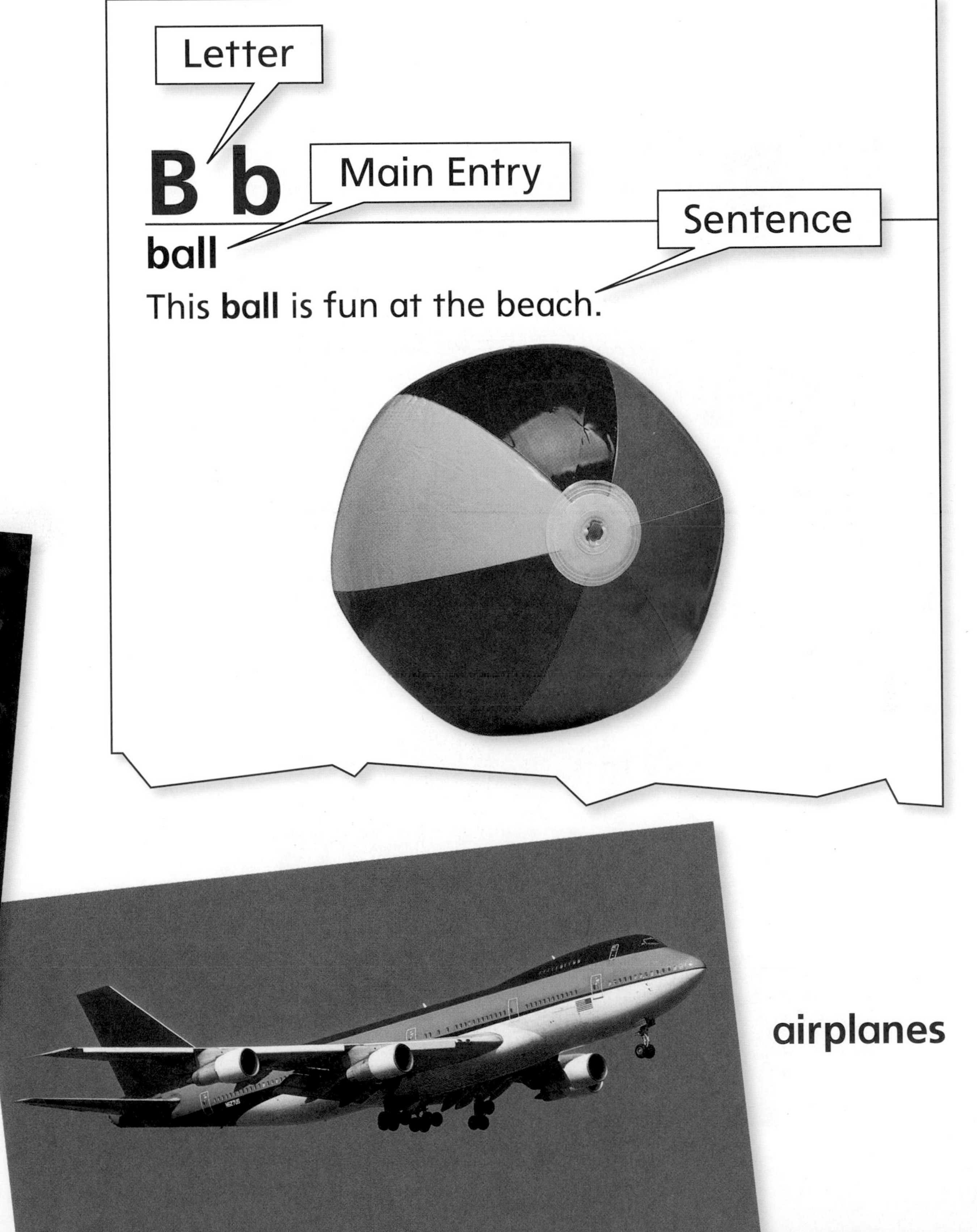

airplanes

Aa

about

Ms. Dunne told us a story **about** ducks.

across

Mike walked **across** the bridge.

airplanes

Airplanes can go very fast.

also

I like to bake bread and **also** eat it.

Bb

ball

This **ball** is fun
at the beach.

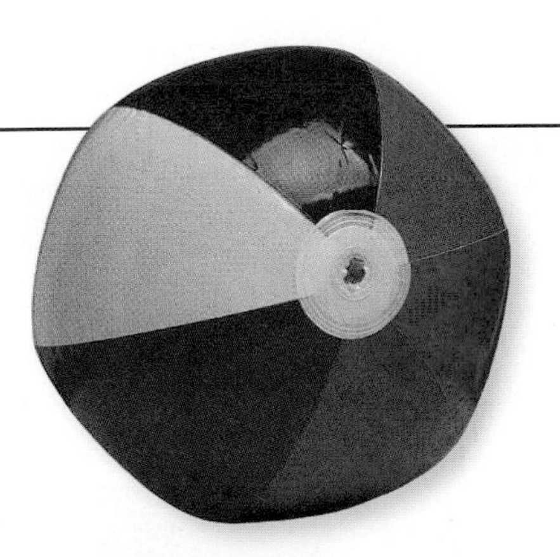

beautiful

Mary's painting is **beautiful**.

because

It's time to leave **because** the movie is over.

better

Greg likes apples **better** than pears.

blue

The sky looks so **blue** today.

borrow

I **borrow** books from the library.

buy

If you **buy** shoes, make sure they fit.

Cc

carry

This animal can **carry** her baby on her back.

celebrate

We **celebrate** Thanksgiving with a big family dinner.

change
The traffic light will soon **change** from red to green.

concentrate
I need to **concentrate** when I read.

Dd

danger
When the cat wakes up, the mouse will be in **danger**.

difficult
It's **difficult** to stand like this.

Ee

eight
When will you become **eight** years old?

Gg

give

It is nice to **give** gifts.

Hh

head

Keisha wears a helmet to protect her **head**.

honey

Honey is sweet and sticky.

Ii

invent

I wish I could **invent** a robot to make my bed.

Mm

machine

A **machine** can help sew clothes.

meadow

The **meadow** is full of flowers.

move

If I **move**, so does my shadow.

Nn

never

Ruby **never** goes to sleep without a story.

Oo

once

Once dinosaurs walked the Earth.

or

Is the kitten bigger **or** smaller than the dog?

other

Sarah ran and the **other** kids walked.

Pp

parade

Everyone dressed up for the **parade**.

perhaps

Perhaps the sun will come out later.

pretty

The fireworks were very **pretty**.

Qq

queen

The **queen** wore a golden crown.

Rr

relatives

Aunt Sally and Uncle Gene are my favorite **relatives**.

ripe

If the peaches are **ripe**, we'll pick them.

Ss

saw

We **saw** three frogs in the pond.

says

My sister **says** she will be late.

should

You **should** eat a good lunch.

shout

I **shout** when I'm happy.

splendid

What a **splendid** day for a picnic!

Tt

trip

We had a great time on our camping **trip**.

Uu

until

Don't run **until** you hear the starting bell.

upon

My grandfather rested his head **upon** the pillow.

Ww

walked

We **walked** to school today.

were

What grade **were** you in last year?

worker

Worker bees build the hive.

write

I **write** with a pencil.

The publisher gratefully acknowledges permission to reprint the following copyrighted material:

"The Kite" from *Days with Frog and Toad* by Arnold Lobel. Text and illustrations copyright © 1979 by Arnold Lobel. Reprinted by permission of Harper & Row Publishers, Inc.

"Where?" from *Seasons: A Book of Poems* by Charlotte Zolotow. Text copyright © 2002 by Charlotte Zolotow. Reprinted by permission of HarperCollins.

Book Cover, FROG AND TOAD ARE FRIENDS by Arnold Lobel. Copyright © 1970 by Arnold Lobel. Reprinted by permission of HarperCollins Publishers.

Book Cover, GRANDPA'S FACE by Eloise Greenfield, illustrated by Floyd Cooper. Text copyright © 1996 by Eloise Greenfield. Illustrations copyright © 1996 by Floyd Cooper. Reprinted by permission of Penguin Putnam Books for Young Readers.

Book Cover, OWL AT HOME by Arnold Lobel. Copyright © 1975 by Arnold Lobel. Reprinted by permission of HarperCollins Children's Books, a division of HarperCollins Publishers.

Book Cover, WHEN WILL I READ? by Miriam Cohen, illustrated by Lillian Hoban. Text copyright © 1977 by Miriam Cohen. Illustrations Copyright © 1977 by Lillian Hoban. Reprinted by permission of Greenwillow Books.

ILLUSTRATIONS

Cover Illustration: Mary Jane Begin

8–9: Sheree Boyd. 10–29: Richard Bernal. 34: Daniel DelValle. 38–39: Patrice Barton. 40–59: Floyd Cooper. 64: Daniel DelValle. 80: Mindy Pierce. 84–85: Jamie Smith. 86–101: Arnold Lobel. 108–109: Ken Bowser. 134–135: Holly Hannon. 138–140: Jannie Ho.

PHOTOGRAPHY

All Photographs are by Ken Cavanagh or Ken Karp for Macmillan/McGraw Hill (MMH) except as noted below.

Inside front & back covers: Robert Glusic/Getty Images. v: (t) Larry Bones/AGE Fotostock;(b) Dana Hursey/Masterfile. 2-3: Roy Botterell/CORBIS. 3: Blend/Getty Images. 4: Blend/PunchStock. 5: Bettmann/CORBIS. 6-7: Jim Cummins/Getty Images. 28: Courtesy of Richard Bernall. 30: Robert C. Hermes/Photo Researchers. 31: (t) Ted Horowitz/CORBIS; (cl) Jan Rietz/Getty Images. 32: John B Free/Nature Picture Library. 33: Papilio/Alamy. 34: Artiga/Masterfile. 35: Eyewire/PunchStock. 36-37: Walter Hodges/Getty Images. 58: (cr) Courtesy of Miriam Cohen; (cl) Courtesy of Floyd Cooper. 60: A.Ramey/Photo Edit. 61: (tr) Laura Dwight/Omni-Photo Communications Inc.; (b) Brand X Pictures/Picture Quest/Jupiter Images. 62: (c) Lawrence Migdale/Photo Researchers; (cl) Michael Newman/Photo Edit; (cr) Phil Schermeister/CORBIS. 63: (t) Ted Streshinsky/CORBIS; (cr) Nik Wheeler/CORBIS. 64: Juice Images/Alamy. 65: Photodisc/Alamy. 66-67: Larry Bones/AGE Fotostock. 68: Mark Thomas/Jupiter Images. 69: Jeff Greenburg/Photo Edit. 70: CSU Archives/Everett Collection. 71: Jupiter Images/Agence Images/Alamy. 72: AP Photo. 73: Wisconsin Historical Society/Courtesy Everett Collection. 74: Jason Laure/The Image Works. 75: AP Photo/Barry Sweet. 76: Arthur Schatz/Time Life Pictures/Getty Images. 78: Jeff Greenburg/The Image Works. 79: (l to r) Action Plus/Alamy; Mikhail Kondrashov/fotomik/Alamy; ClassicStock/Alamy. 80: Corbis/PunchStock. 82-83: image100/Alamy. 100: Courtesy of Arnold Lobel. 102: Underwood & Underwood/CORBIS. 102-103: Stockbyte/Getty Images. 103: Underwood & Underwood/CORBIS. 104: CORBIS. 104-105: (bkgd) Stockbyte/Getty Images. 105: National Archives/Handout/Getty Images. 106: CORBIS. 106-107: Stockbyte/Getty Images. 107: (tl, tc, tr) Photodisc/Getty Images; (bl, br) Digital Vision/Getty Images; (bc) PhotoLink/Getty Images. 108: Darren Greenwood/Alamy. 110-111: Tui de Roy/Minden Pictures. 112-113: Fred Bavendam/Animals Animals. 114-115: Dana Hursey/Masterfile. 116: Photodisc/PunchStock. 117: Georgette Douwma/Photo Researchers. 118-119: Tony Heald/Nature Picture Library. 120-121: Images&Stories/Alamy. 121: Gary Bell/Oceanwideimages.com. 122-123: Karen Tweedy-Holmes/CORBIS. 123: Digital Vision/PunchStock. 124: FRED BAVENDAM /Minden Pictures. 124-125: Stuart Westmorland/CORBIS. 126: Arco Images/Alamy. 127: (t) Valerie Giles/Photo Researchers; (b) Rick & Nora Bowers/Alamy. 128: (t) CARL ROESSLER/Animals Animals. 128-129: Fred Bavendam/Minden Pictures. 130-131: Gerard Lacz/Peter Arnold, Inc. 132: (tr) Courtesy of Julia Smith; (c) Rick & Nora Bowers/Alamy. 133: (bl) Karen Tweedy-Holmes/CORBIS; (br) Photodisc/PunchStock. 136: Iconica/Getty Images. 137: G.K. & Vicki Hart/Getty Images. 140: Anup Shah/Getty Images. 141: BIRGIT KOCH/Animals Animals. 144: Gary Bell/zefa/CORBIS. 145: (t) Stockbyte/PunchStock; (b) imageshop - zefa visual media uk ltd/Alamy. 146: (t) BananaStock/Alamy; (b) imageshop - zefa visual media uk ltd/Alamy. 147: (t) Stockbyte/PunchStock; (b) William Manning/CORBIS. 148: (t) Gary Bell/zefa/CORBIS; (b) Paul Barton/CORBIS. 150: (t) David Schmidt/Masterfile; (b) Rommel/Masterfile. 151: (t) Digital Vision/PunchStock; (b) Tetra Images/PunchStock. 152: (t) Paul Freytag/zefa/CORBIS; (b) Masterfile Royalty Free. 153: (t) Helga Lade/Peter Arnold; (b) LHB Photo/Alamy. 154: Dynamic Graphics Group/Creatas/Alamy. 155: CORBIS. 156: Banana Stock/AGE Fotostock. 157: (t) Masterfile Royalty Free; (b) LWA-Sharie Kennedy/CORBIS. CA Standards pages 1-4: Medioimages/PunchStock.

Reading/Language Arts
CA California Standards
Grade 1

READING

1.0 Word Analysis, Fluency, and Systematic Vocabulary Development
Students understand the basic features of reading. They select letter patterns and know how to translate them into spoken language by using phonics, syllabication, and word parts. They apply this knowledge to achieve fluent oral and silent reading.

Concepts About Print

1.1	Match oral words to printed words.
1.2	Identify the title and author of a reading selection.
1.3	Identify letters, words, and sentences.

Phonemic Awareness

1.4	Distinguish initial, medial, and final sounds in single-syllable words.
1.5	Distinguish long-and short-vowel sounds in orally stated single-syllable words (e.g., *bit/bite)*.
1.6	Create and state a series of rhyming words, including consonant blends.
1.7	Add, delete, or change target sounds to change words (e.g., change *cow* to *how; pan* to *an)*.
1.8	Blend two to four phonemes into recognizable words (e.g., */c/ a/ t/* = cat; */f/ l/ a/ t/* = flat).
1.9	Segment single-syllable words into their components (e.g., */c/ a/ t/* = cat; */s/ p/ l/ a/ t/* = splat; */r/ i/ ch/* = rich).

Decoding and Word Recognition

1.10	Generate the sounds from all the letters and letter patterns, including consonant blends and long-and short-vowel patterns (i.e., phonograms), and blend those sounds into recognizable words.
1.11	Read common, irregular sight words (e.g., *the, have, said, come, give, of)*.
1.12	Use knowledge of vowel digraphs and *r-* controlled letter-sound associations to read words.
1.13	Read compound words and contractions.
1.14	Read inflectional forms (e.g., *-s, -ed, -ing)* and root words (e.g., *look, looked, looking)*.
1.15	Read common word families (e.g., *-ite, -ate)*.
1.16	Read aloud with fluency in a manner that sounds like natural speech.

Vocabulary and Concept Development

1.17 Classify grade-appropriate categories of words (e.g., concrete collections of animals, foods, toys).

2.0 **Reading Comprehension**
Students read and understand grade-level-appropriate material. They draw upon a variety of comprehension strategies as needed (e.g., generating and responding to essential questions, making predictions, comparing information from several sources). The selections in *Recommended Literature, Kindergarten Through Grade Twelve* illustrate the quality and complexity of the materials to be read by students. In addition to their regular school reading, by grade four, students read one-half million words annually, including a good representation of grade-level-appropriate narrative and expository text (e.g., classic and contemporary literature, magazines, newspapers, online information). In grade one, students begin to make progress toward this goal.

Structural Features of Informational Materials

2.1 Identify text that uses sequence or other logical order.

Comprehension and Analysis of Grade-Level-Appropriate Text

2.2 Respond to *who, what, when, where,* and *how* questions.

2.3 Follow one-step written instructions.

2.4 Use context to resolve ambiguities about word and sentence meanings.

2.5 Confirm predictions about what will happen next in a text by identifying key words (i.e., signpost words).

2.6 Relate prior knowledge to textual information.

2.7 Retell the central ideas of simple expository or narrative passages.

3.0 **Literary Response and Analysis** Students read and respond to a wide variety of significant works of children's literature. They distinguish between the structural features of the text and the literary terms or elements (e.g., theme, plot, setting, characters). The selections in *Recommended Literature, Kindergarten Through Grade Twelve* illustrate the quality and complexity of the materials to be read by students.

Narrative Analysis of Grade-Level-Appropriate Text

3.1 Identify and describe the elements of plot, setting, and character(s) in a story, as well as the story's beginning, middle, and ending.

3.2 Describe the roles of authors and illustrators and their contributions to print materials.

3.3 Recollect, talk, and write about books read during the school year.

WRITING

1.0 **Writing Strategies** Students write clear and coherent sentences and paragraphs that develop a central idea. Their writing shows they consider the audience and purpose. Students progress through the stages of the writing process (e.g., prewriting, drafting, revising, editing successive versions).

Organization and Focus

1.1 Select a focus when writing.

1.2 Use descriptive words when writing.

Penmanship

1.3 Print legibly and space letters, words, and sentences appropriately.

2.0 **Writing Applications (Genres and Their Characteristics)** Students write compositions that describe and explain familiar objects, events, and experiences. Student writing demonstrates a command of standard American English and the drafting, research, and organizational strategies outlined in Writing Standard 1.0.
Using the writing strategies of grade one outlined in Writing Standard 1.0, students:

2.1 Write brief narratives (e.g., fictional, autobiographical) describing an experience.

2.2 Write brief expository descriptions of a real object, person, place, or event, using sensory details.

WRITTEN AND ORAL ENGLISH LANGUAGE CONVENTIONS

The standards for written and oral English language conventions have been placed between those for writing and for listening and speaking because these conventions are essential to both sets of skills.

1.0 **Written and Oral English Language Conventions** Students write and speak with a command of standard English conventions appropriate to this grade level.

Sentence Structure

1.1 Write and speak in complete, coherent sentences.

Grammar

1.2 Identify and correctly use singular and plural nouns.

1.3 Identify and correctly use contractions (e.g., *isn't, aren't, can't, won't)* and singular possessive pronouns (e.g., *my/ mine, his/ her, hers, your/s)* in writing and speaking.

Punctuation	
1.4	Distinguish between declarative, exclamatory, and interrogative sentences.
1.5	Use a period, exclamation point, or question mark at the end of sentences.
1.6	Use knowledge of the basic rules of punctuation and capitalization when writing.
Capitalization	
1.7	Capitalize the first word of a sentence, names of people, and the pronoun *I*.
Spelling	
1.8	Spell three-and four-letter short-vowel words and grade-level-appropriate sight words correctly.

LISTENING AND SPEAKING

1.0 **Listening and Speaking Strategies** Students listen critically and respond appropriately to oral communication. They speak in a manner that guides the listener to understand important ideas by using proper phrasing, pitch, and modulation.

Comprehension	
1.1	Listen attentively.
1.2	Ask questions for clarification and understanding.
1.3	Give, restate, and follow simple two-step directions.
Organization and Delivery of Oral Communication	
1.4	Stay on the topic when speaking.
1.5	Use descriptive words when speaking about people, places, things, and events.

2.0 **Speaking Applications (Genres and Their Characteristics)** Students deliver brief recitations and oral presentations about familiar experiences or interests that are organized around a coherent thesis statement. Student speaking demonstrates a command of standard American English and the organizational and delivery strategies outlined in Listening and Speaking Standard 1.0.

Using the speaking strategies of grade one outlined in Listening and Speaking Standard 1.0, students:

2.1	Recite poems, rhymes, songs, and stories.
2.2	Retell stories using basic story grammar and relating the sequence of story events by answering *who, what, when, where, why,* and *how* questions.
2.3	Relate an important life event or personal experience in a simple sequence.
2.4	Provide descriptions with careful attention to sensory detail.